MORE FROM
THE FALCON'S NEST

MORE FROM
THE FALCON'S
NEST

Bromyard Poetry for Pleasure Group

More From the Falcon's Nest
Compiled by Bryony Cullum, with help from other members,
for the Bromyard Poetry for Pleasure Group

Published by Aspect Design 2018
Malvern, Worcestershire, United Kingdom.

Designed, printed and bound by Aspect Design
89 Newtown Road, Malvern, Worcs. WR14 1PD
United Kingdom
Tel: 01684 561567
E-mail: allan@aspect-design.net
Website: www.aspect-design.net

Cover Design Copyright © 2018 Aspect Design
Original photograph Copyright © Denis R.H. Teal 2018
ISBN 978-1-912078-94-3

CONTENTS

PREFACE

HEREFORDSHIRE

SEASONS

FAMILY – LIFE – PEOPLE

CHILDREN'S POETRY

THE NATURAL WORLD

HUMOUR

SHORT POEMS AND HAIKUS

ABROAD

HISTORY – WAR

RELIGION, PHILOSOPHICAL, MISCELLANEOUS

BROMYARD POET'S CHRISTMAS DINNER

PREFACE

Fifteen years ago, two friends – Ann Dolan and I - decided to create 'Poetry for Pleasure' to explore our wonderful heritage of poetry and bring it to Bromyard and the surrounding district.

Three poetry books later, and with an annual Children's Poetry Competition and a monthly visit to an old people's home, we certainly are fulfilling that early aspiration.

Since our last book we have lost two of our writers, John Elmes and Charles Gordon Clark. They were valued members of our group. Their characters live on in their poetry, which we are lucky to share, among ourselves, and with you.

We write, learn and sometimes just read poetry. The Group meets at 7.30pm on the first Wednesday of each month (apart from August) in Falcon Mews at The Falcon Hotel, Bromyard (the old theatre projection room). Our falcon's nest – or eyrie! Everyone is welcome.

We thought a fitting title for our book would be 'More from the Falcon's Nest'.

Margaret Dallow

Co-founder and Chair of Bromyard Poetry for Pleasure

We should like to thank Sylvia and John and their staff
for their support in all our activities.

HEREFORDSHIRE

BROMYARD – HISTORIC MARKET TOWN

Dried grass fans the sign in bold print
spelling the town ahead among the folding hills,
homes crisscross in brick and stone,
on a greater age their footings stand.
Gone the corrugated sheds and pens;
in place a leisure centre sits, brooding like a red fat hen.
Come Thursdays saw the farming folk to town,
gossiping down streets broad and high,
the ample wives elbowing willow baskets, filled with brown eggs,
butter yellow as the sunny celandine.

A plethora of pub signs swinging in the breeze,
glasses foam with golden beer,
'til the tawny owl called from dusky woods.
Blue haze hung about the snugs and bars,
quaffers merry, making trading deals.

Ironmongers, 'Maynes' and 'Pettifers' outside
stacked their shiny pails,
spouted cans for paraffin, the hard yard brooms.
About the square stalls with chinaware,
in striped apron the fish-man plied,
'Come buy my herrings, ladies dear,
fresh mackerel netted in the rolling sea,
tasty kippers smoked on oak
a special treat for all your teas.'

The farmer on stout hazel leans,
wind-worn cheek, knee bent,
his faithful collie at his feet;
debates the vagaries of hops,
Goldings, Fuggles and the dreaded wilt.
In other times of quiet beasts they spoke,
harnessed to the plough, and heavy horse,
slicing straight furrows through fertile fields.
Under open sky lay the market yard,
Herefords bellowing in their pens
white sows grunting to piglets suckling,
their curly tails brought smiles to the watching child.

In Harris Tweed the auctioneer stands,
firing bids from his lofty perch,
a decibel above the bleat of yearling lambs.
Sheared ewes' crimson fate
awaits in Rowberry Street.

The day draws the evening in, and parcel-laden folk
seek home by Church Street to the train,
on Burnham's bus or Jones' of Highlane.
And in the slanting shadows' hush,
still and silent are those market pens,
beneath a glow of yellow neon,
the last man is going home.

Charles Gordon Clark, 1936-2018.

VISITING DAY –
AT LOWER BROCKHAMPTON MANOR HOUSE

On this soft blue day
our visitors will come,
to view Brockhampton's medieval charm.
Lime-washed fresh in winter past,
over white walls crimson roses spill.
Behind the diamond leaded windows
a simple history lies.

From cool flagstone porch I scan
Herefords cropping summer grass,
their calves suckle content.
A new herd bred again,
after fires of that other spring.
I see the wind weave silver wheat,
earth's green lungs spread out,
beech, broad oak and slender birch,
and the woodland paths they shade.

Here swallows swoop and loop,
feeding their chicks in adobe nests
built beneath the Gate House eaves.
Old medlar tree still bears its ugly fruit,
and rosemary scents by open door.
Mallards, on the moat,
quack among the lily pads;
their ducklings paddle close,
for mink and fox hide near,
await silence and the night.

I turn and welcome all,
who wish to wander here.

Josie Ann Dolan.

BROMYARD GLOVES

Just off the main street
in our small town,
there in the old vinegar factory,
I am told,
gloves were made
of every hue:
reseda green, cyclamen, marina blue,
sadly no longer sold.

Satin, suede, leather too,
machined and tested
by fresh faced girls with tightly
curled hair and overalls of brown.
Singing along to Mario Lanza
happy and laughing,
out they would spill,
down to the café at the end of the lane.

How privileged we felt to own
just one pair.
Weddings and gloves
were fashionable then.

Just a memory now.
Smart gloves, so lovingly made,
one more thing
at which Bromyard excelled.

Margaret Dallow.

WALK ON WAPLEY HILL FORT

Passing on the Presteigne Road
I noted the sign to Wapley Hill,
and remembered being told
it's good for bluebells and bird life,
and determined to go one day.

One day was yesterday,
a spring day – one like summer;
blue skies, light white clouds,
really warm sunshine, but in May.

We looked at the Forestry Commission's board.
The map outlined a moderate walk.
The mown path enticed us.
The wild flowers entranced us –
campion, stitchwort, bluebells, violets.

We saw glimpses of colourful countryside,
Herefordians' patchwork fields
ploughed or bright with rape,
hedges in spring green and white.

We frequently stopped
to admire and get our breath.
No embarrassment for this unfit pair,
time to notice dapples.
We explored the variety of mosses, ferns and conifers,
the various ages and styles of planting;
plantations, coppicing, avenues of beech, mixed woodland,
each with their own atmosphere.

Our strongest challenge the northern edge:
it had to be climbed to reach the Fort.
Such a reward awaited us –
brilliant yellow broom set among bluebells
backed by cloudless sky; man-made ramparts
clothed verdant green by nature,
the aerial view quite overwhelming.

We spared thoughts for those who had laboured,
endured wild winter winds and bitter cold,
maybe anxious for their future.

Our overall impressions:
the absorbable peace of the place,
filtered sunshine,
snatches of vistas,
venerable oaks,
blackbirds' accompaniment.

Our last impressions –
thankfulness and joy.

Bryony Cullum, May 2018.

THE CIRCUS CAME TO TOWN

Enquiring trunks,
doors shut firmly –
shared memories
of when the circus came to town.

Dancing ponies,
runaway bears,
the monkey that ran off
with the washing.

Circus life forever unfolding
here in our sleepy streets,
in the dark days
of the Second World War.

Tales still told
in the pubs,
how the elephants sadly died
and were buried in a field nearby.

The three stools
on which the elephants performed
found dusty and rotting
in a high street cellar.

With names barely legible,
Winkey, Blinkey and Nod
from a nursery rhyme
once told,

shared amongst the people
born and bred
in our little market town.
Stories that are folklore now.

Margaret Dallow.

WEST NORTH and EAST

We moved here quite some time ago
with all our worldly goods in tow,
to run a place of rest for chaps
with mint cake in their walking sacks.

Coming over Frome's Hill's rise
a glorious sight then met our eyes,
with fish bowl sloshing between my feet,
the laid out patchwork made our happiness complete.

Victorian building, red brick and strong,
we knew we'd arrived where we belonged.
Sheep dealer's Will had given all to charity –
buildings, land and yearly gratuity.

This grand house was now our home,
to care for the structure and the folks who roamed.
We baked and cleaned, and sold them tins
of beans and meat, and other things.

This beautiful county which not many know
is the place that we chose for our children to grow.
'Escape to the Country' will give away clues
as to why we few love the lanes and the views.

We enabled others to feast on the sights,
the sounds of the rivers, the vales and the heights,
the colours, the quiet, the fields and still
Herefordshire's beauty continues to thrill.

We stayed as do many who've found this delight.
We've moved, but only to prove ourselves right,

that west, north or east this county is best,
and we'll probably stay for our eternal rest!

Maggie McGladdery.

Bromyard Gala, by Denis Teal

THE BROMYARD GALA 2005

The Gala born again
on Bromyard's ancient parkland.
Galloping Horses, a Ferris Wheel,
rides from a bygone age
stand proud against the sky.

On plastic chair Granny sits,
Queen of this gypsy tribe.
Old now but useful still
takes money for a ride.
Children clutching square hemp mats
climb the stairs,
come shouting and laughing
down the slide.

Gypsy Rose leaves her smart address
where kings and queens dwell.
Crystal balls of different sizes
catch sunbeams on her window sill.

Painted wagons here on show,
admired and marvelled at.
Gypsies from another land –
no painted wagons now –
tell that the 'babby's' ill –
an age-old tale.

Evening now the Gala breathes
one last breath, egg throwing.
A round-face boy in Romany speaks –
presses pennies in my hand.
Father with leather skin,
hair as black as raven wing,
leans against a post and says,
'GOOD GALA'.

Margaret Dallow.

HEREFORD CATHEDRAL
Frozen Music

In the year of our Lord 1080 the foundation stone was laid,
in decades to come from boulders of stone, square building blocks
were made,
stone masons by the dozen and labourers by the score,
from the breaking of the day to the dawning of the night their
labours came to the fore.
As stone from the quarries and timber from our forests were
floated down the Wye,
stout larch poles for scaffolding and strong hemp rope for which
to tie.
Over the years this house of God began to take its place as a
monument of beauty in our shire;
as the centuries pass by its awesome splendour never ceases to
inspire.
On entering through the northern porch and standing beneath
the massive Norman piers
as folk from every walk of life and every corner of the globe have
done for many, many years,
enveloped in this spiritual splendour when looking at
King Stephen's chair carved of local timber
in the year of 1138 and looking as good as it's ever been,
and twice in her record reign
has been the seat of our own
beloved Queen.
It houses some of the treasures of our country, the 'Chained
Library', and the ancient Mappa Mundi;
the grand old font carved out by the Normans in the year 1150
stands as a monument to the past;

ornate towers and polished pews, massive bells, and stout oak
doors only time will outlast.
As the sun rises over the eastern tower standing there alone,
reflections in the rippling Wye – it's like a symphony set in stone.
If future generations return to dust, the Maestro lowers his
baton, the orchestra ceases to play
when the moon and stars fail to reign over the night and the sun
doesn't light up the day,
Will this house of God defiantly stand? No one knows – it's hard
to say.

Denis R.H. Teal.

Photo, by Denis Teal, of Hereford Cathedral at time of Rememberance 2018,
showing the "Weeping Window"

WIGMORE ABBEY

We turned the corner,
tyres squelching on farmyard mud.
There it was, the ancient Abbey,
lights twinkling from windows high above.

Down the steps to the cellar
the studded door swings open;
feet clatter on uneven slabs –
a glass of wine and friends well met.

Through a slither of a door
into a cavern painted now of ochre gold.
A fire crackles and spits;
who sat by that hearth of old?

Tales of battles and treachery
and unrequited loves
were told as candles fluttered
and shadows grew.

Ancient spirits mingle and drift,
female voices rise and fall,
the dulcimer peels out
where the abbots' wine was stored.

We leave into the cold winter night
feeling the heritage of the borders
swirling round our heads –
the spirits now drift back into the stone-built walls.

Margaret Dallow.

HOME THOUGHTS FROM FORMER HOMES

If I were back in Surrey now
what would I miss from that western shire?
Tall perry trees and mistletoe.

If I were once again in Kent
what would I wish were still around?
Hop-yards flourish in Hereford.

If I were in sound of Oxford's bells
what views would the meadows by Isis lack?
Malverns to south, Clee north, Wales west.

If I were back where my pram was wheeled
flowers would be missing in Battersea Park
Stockings Meadow has cowslip sheets,
meadow saffron hides on the Doward,
yellow rattle clothes Bromyard Downs.

So I think I'll stay in Herefordshire,
for the earth is red in Herefordshire,
and the Hereford cattle troop from the byre,
and the orchards cover the ground like a fleece,
and the hills and the woods are a dream of peace.

Charles Gordon Clark.

AFTER THE JUBILEE

Why does the village seem so quiet and dull?
The school and hall are no longer full.
Telephones silent – notes put aside,
committee members scattered wide.

The flags are down, the people away.
The stalls all empty, no art on display.
All put away but still talked about.
A great success? Without a doubt.

Judy Malet.

SEASONS

SPRING AT THE WEIR

Afternoon shaded walk, late May, warm sunshine,
the trees are wearing their bright spring coats.
The mighty plane's girth betrays its age, 300 years.
In its limbs the rooks have built their homes.

The lime green tips of the Douglas fir proclaim its renewal;
sweet chestnuts are bright with white and rosy plumes.

I sit upon the grassy bank, bordered by wildflowers and rushes.
Branches straddling the edges of the river
gracefully bow to lightly touch
from where it receives its life.

Proud mother swan with brood effortlessly rides the fast-flowing water.
My eyes lift to the terraces of this garden by the Wye
where all the hues of spring are on display.
Life renewed.

The Weir Swainshill
Rosemarie J. Powell, 2015.

APRIL AND THE POETS
An Extended Sonnet

April! So what then do the poets say?
"The uncertain glory of an April day" –
Shakespeare of course – a phrase of simple beauty
where lack of detail is the line of duty.

Not so for Browning; but for him excuse
is distance, memory's needs, a simple ruse
to give familiar sights and sounds a change,
so that we see them new, exotic, strange.

A different angle, centuries before,
not, 'What's April?' but, 'What's April for?'
For holidays, says Chaucer, ever sage,
"Then longen folk to go on pilgrimage".
But when your theme is the Waste Land
April's fecundity is hard to stand:
"The cruellest month", writes Eliot; breeding
must make uncomfortable reading;
lilacs or lilies, April can't stay quiet:
new growth insists each year on April riot.

Charles Gordon Clark, 2017.

SUMMER

Sounds of summer remembered with nostalgia:
evocative sounds – the kraark krowk of lawn mowers every Sunday;
cricket balls smacking against willow, John Arlot heard on the radio;
stanzas of buzz...es from bees and other insects;
a crash of thunder and pounding raindrops;
high-pitched voices of children as families enjoy the sea;
just a whisper of breezes shuffling leaves.
How gladly we shed our winter woollies,
expose our sun-creamed skin to the sun.
Seek for cool and easy-wear clothes,
allow our toes to peep through sandals;
become hot and sweaty, long for shade or air conditioning.

Summer – our change of life style.
Daylight wakes us up and dusk allows us to linger.
Our diet alters from stews and puddings
to colourful salads and ice creams.

We marvel at the profusion of flowers
as we change from cold, gloomy grey days
to blue skies, scudding clouds and sunshine.

There are fewer hazards and cancellations;
we are more optimistic and cheerful.

Let us enjoy this summer.
Relax, breathe, and read.
Let sounds and music caress us
as the swifts and swallows, chittering, swirl overhead.

Bryony Cullum, May 2018.

SONGS AND CHARABANCS

The yard was cleaned out
where cattle had wintered;
barracks whitewashed –
all must be ready.

The hop-pickers
were coming
from down in the valleys.

Two hundred souls
brought here in the lorries;
another followed behind
with all of the baggage.

Ninety-six children,
their only holiday.
Black tips of coal
make up their mountains.

Songs and charabancs
are my memories.

Busloads of visitors arrive
on a Sunday
potatoes and apples stuffed in a bag.
Father checking
not more than their quota.

Strains of hymns
ring out through the rafters
down that long drive to the farm called Garford.

Margaret Dallow.

MY AUTUMN

Autumn – think apples,
orbs of delight upon the trees;
rich orbs of delight colouring the ground.
A horse hears one drop,
charges over to feed before a rival.
No magnificent Troy on hind legs picking his own.
Sheep greedily crunch, munch,
saliva drips from their mouths.

Each day a problem – what to wear?
Is it summer clothes reclaimed from storage
or, on a grey, cold dull day a need for warmer garments?
As leaves shiver on the trees,
Sandals or boots, bare arms or gloves?

The fledgling swallows, new nesters in the barn,
looking like piecrust holders in their lofty perch
have gone.

Such spectacular colour!
A cherry tree flames into the sky.
Acacia and hazel make yellow patterns, ever deeper,
camouflaging potholes filled with liquid rust reflections.
The silver birch sheens like "Strictly"
as green transforms into gold.

Skeins of bryony adorn the hedgerows.
Grazing sheep weave winding paths
through glittering, shimmering dew.
Hard dry earth softens and clings;
mud again enters our world.

Is there a better autumn pattern
than that done by slugs and snails on cabbage leaves?
How runner beans and raspberries
kid you that none are left!

The rowan entices with scarlet clusters,
bright against a perfect blue, or glowering, sky,
waiting for the winter wave
of fieldfare, redwing, blackbird and others
as we hear news of returning migrants.

Autumn variations give us such a paint box.
We love our greens turning crimson, purple, chestnut, yellow,
which cheer us into the darker days.

Fidget and Ditty, feeling the colder nights
rush to be Yin and Yang, a furry ball on my duvet.
For me it will soon be "hotty botty" time,
a warm bed, a longer read as winter is upon us.

Bryony Cullum, October 2015.

THE HOP DRYER

The night hangs heavy
with the sulphur fumes,
the evening mist gathers
down in the valley.

Drying the hops has begun.
Sacks brought to the kiln,
picked and leafed in ancient cribs,
piled high on the lofty green stage.

Now carefully spread sack by sack
on the kiln's hessian floor
to be dried by oil or coal.
The man in charge is called 'The Dryer'.

He's the man who holds the key
to whether the crop succeeds or fails.
Two loads a day, he never sleeps
eight hours a time
the hops are cooked.

Then you wait
for the load to come back,
a phrase the farmer used.

Cooled and coddled,
finally crushed under pressure
into the giant pockets
proudly stamped with the farmer's name.

We lived and breathed
hops here in the Frome valley.
It was our life, our heritage;
it simply consolidated village life.

It's all but gone –
an old man's memories now.
Will our children ever know
the feeling of a community pulling together?

Margaret Dallow.

A WINTER'S TALE – SNOW MEMORIES

White blanket rising,
making surprising
patterns of lace
in the window-pane race.

Falling and drifting
cold dust like icing
building the drift wedge
over the window ledge.

Told by the weather man
'Stay home if you can',
no sledging, no snow ball –
'Hard rain's a-gonna fall'.

Dark ice by white hedges,
diamonds lengthen from ledges;
frozen beauty and the sun glows
'Everywhere the wind blows'.

Maggie McGladdery.

THE OTHER WINTER'S TALE

Core-numbing, soul-numbing cold
drifting, shifting snow blanket in folds
freezing body flesh
needing comfort and rest.

Concentrate on breathing,
forget about needing.
Dreams of warm smiles,
warm welcomes, no denials.

Intake of air –
short, sharp and spare;
pain leaving,
chest heaving –
and still.

Maggie McGladdery.

ASPECTS OF WINTER

(1)

Sun going down on a winter evening,
clouds turning into multicoloured
kaleidoscopes ... dramatic reds, blacks,
greys, palest pinks, deep purples
stretching across the sky with gay abandon.

Trees naked, stark, reaching upwards,
dark against the skyline.
Black crows roosting on their highest
swaying branches ...
they rise into the air,
circle on the breeze,
returning, settling like late-autumn leaves
reluctant to fall to earth.

(2)

January with its cold, dreary days,
early darkness, feelings of futility.
Each day mundane,
going to bed weary ...
longing for spring.

Seasonal suicides happen,
a sickness blowing on the north wind,
catching the unsuspecting,
undulating dark clouds,
creeping into the hidden
recesses of your mind.

Snowdrops peeping up –
white angels of the spring;
green buds suddenly appearing,
daffodil shoots just showing.
Your spirit rises joyfully
like the sun in the morning.

(3)
Snow-covered mountains,
frozen-over lakes,
trees covered in white,
the air cold and crisp.
Winter sun shining,
sparkling frost abounds,
melting in the sunshine
only to appear once again.
Ducks slipping and sliding
by the riverside, swans
pale against the snow,
and chilly winter skies.

Twinkling lights at nightfall,
showing winter's fairyland;
children throwing snowballs,
building snowmen, scarves flowing,
noses glowing as they criss-cross the street,
hurrying home to warm frozen toes and feet.

(4)
Mountains glowing beneath the winter sun,
pheasants wandering past, richly coloured,
hiding their beauty in the grassy undergrowth,
targets for the shooter's gun.

Iconic sound of birds on the wing,
ducks flying in perfect formation,
the sun catching their soft feathers,
turning them rosy pink as they make their way

to lakes and rivers many miles away.

Intricate black lacy patterns
of trees stretching across the horizon;
cheeky, purply-pink petticoats, frothy and light
showing through their lacy transparency.

The snow when it falls,
glistening in the last of the afternoon sun;
piles of spun sugar
catching colours from every direction.
A giant fir tree throws a shadow
dark against the virgin white,
fading away as the blood red sun
sinks below the horizon.

(5)
Will of the Wind
Weeping willows weeping, bent double,
reaching flowing, choppy water,
dragging their swaying branches
backwards and forwards,
moving to the rhythm
of the wind.

Clouds racing across the river,
chasing ripples to the other side.
Water versus cloud
as they dance together
for our amusement.

A feeling of exhilaration,
running against the wind,
its strength holding you back,
gusting in your face,
making it tingle, leaving you
gasping for breath.

A battle of wills
that can't be won.
Invigorating, exciting
as nature and you
bow to the will of the wind.

Jane Dallow, 2011 and 2012.

FAMILY – LIFE – PEOPLE

BIRTH DAY POEM
With acknowledgement to Anne Bradstreet (1612-72)

If ever two were one then surely we –
minute beginnings inside of me
microscopic –
growing, gradually –
slowly, inexorably – inevitably –
increasing, developing, the new life within,
stretching my skin,
which envelops your growth;
anticipation, preparation,
excitement grows with you.

Now wearing, exhausting, transporting
every morsel I ingest,
every drink I imbibe, inside
whatever I do
transfers to you.

Then – perhaps now stretched too far
we, who are two – together
begin to part.
The leaving is hard –
we have been one for so long –
used to each other – cohesive – combined.

Now expand – contract
to end the contract
expand – contract – expletive – repeat;
then relief – and welcome –
the meeting, the greeting.
I know you!
and a new expansion begins.

If ever one were two, then surely we;
now you are free.

Maggie McGladdery.

CHRISTOPHER (Aged 3½)

Christopher, small as yet to carry but within
that radiance not of man's creation:
framed without by mix of red and blue,
and multi-coloured welly-boots;
by sun-touched tousled hair to edge
that disproportionate but appropriate forehead,
and that oh-so-mobile mouth,

almost too eloquent for three-and-forty months;
small, earnest, energetic lovable bundle
of fun and exploration.

John Pare, May 1981.

Chris is now a barrister!

HYMN TO HADEEQA

Welcome to the world, Hadeeqa;
right now you're a little squeaker
but you'll moderate quite soon!
Sorry you were kept inside there;
were you quite content to hide there?
Are you, like us, o'er the moon?

We like you a lot, Hadeeqa,
glad that you weren't any weaker
for your longer stay inside.
Outside seems a little scary
and it's right you should be wary,
as the world seems very wide.

You are suckling now, Hadeeqa –
one day you will use a beaker –
so don't run before you walk.
Your small lungs are getting practice
and we all know that the fact is
in no time you'll start to talk!

You're a bright spark, dear Hadeeqa,
and no doubt you'll be a seeker
after knowledge, after truth;
you'll be brought up well, we know it
(p'raps you'll also be a poet!)
through your childhood and your youth.

Of this we are sure, Hadeeka,
you will never be a geek, a
nerd, or other sort of fool.
You have got a start to dream of,
trav'lling's sure to be the theme of
life for you; it will be cool.

You'll find out, minute Hadeeqa,
as you grow, some think life bleaker
than it really is in fact.
If you ever get downhearted
turn to those who haven't parted
from their hopes; is that a pact?

John Pare, March 2012.

The above was written just after Hadeeqa was born two weeks overdue in
Sri Lanka to my second son and his Muslim wife (hence the unusual name).
She is once again in Sri Lanka as a beautiful, lively six-year-old. She may
shortly be moving to live in New Zealand.

MY BOY

I wrote this poem about my son Tom in 2008. He is now 26 and lives and works in the centre of London. I'm happy to say he still has all the same good qualities but is now tidy, organised and extremely hard working!

He was born on a sunny Sunday morning,
early October, golden light.
At that moment I knew I was his forever.
A tidal wave of new love hit me,
left me reeling.
My boy –
an ordinary miracle,
a glimpse of heaven.

My boy is seventeen now;
loving, kind, funny, caring,
untidy, impractical, disorganised,
brave, generous, loyal and friendly,
a master of mimic and timing.
The world is a better place
because my boy is in it.

Dorothy Kennedy.

TODAY SHE HELD MY HAND

The best of being Granny
was falling in love
all over again –
the miracle without the pain.

The best of being Granny:
without exhaustion
at the end of the day
is having time to play.

Now we have our moments,
will against will,
but I don't have to win;
Granny can give in.

The best of going shopping
is what will she do?
walk on walls, jump off steps,
adventure unplanned;
but today she held my hand.

Thalia Gordon Clark.

ANOTHER GOODBYE

My mind recalls the day you stood
looking down on the old hometown.

Clouds lie low
in the western sky,
grey and blue.

Stretching your arms wide,
taking with you for comfort on your journey –
one this time I cannot share.

Lost in the sound of the gentle wind whispering
in the trees over Warren Wood.

Rosemarie J. Powell, spring 2008.

Returning to one of the places that my late sister held dearly.

ALONE NOW

The green mug I used for your morning coffee
sits pointedly on the draining-board,
testament to your presence then
and your absence now;

The knitted maroon dress you often wear in bed
on colder nights lies on the armchair,
for it was warm at the weekend
and you wore cotton;

The slippers I bought you soon after you first came
lie reproachfully by the dressing table,
as if to say, 'Why are we not of use;
why is she not here?'.

Your toiletries cluster on the bathroom windowsill,
with more on the floor on your side
of the bed we so enjoy together,
but look unused.

Your spare glasses on the coffee table in their case
await the opportunity to read the paper,
but must wait a longer time now
to be of any use.

Your quilted jacket hangs on the porch peg,
visible whenever I exit or enter,
all of these quotidian things
marking your absence.

I sit here alone,
though on Sunday, together,
we breakfasted side-by-side, happy
but already talking of the sadness of our parting.

John Pare, May 2017.

MAKING THE BED

Tubby Turner's mother died making the bed.
They found her kneeling, bent, with a sheet
   ready to be tucked in, a blanket lying
   calmly at the foot, the pillows plumped,
rubber bottle drained of last night's warmth.

Sun dazzled the January windows.
The wireless burbled 'Woman's Hour' and 'Morning Story'.
The dogs began scratching the kitchen door.
The pigs in the yard ran hungry and squealing.
The chickens pecked each other in frustration –

while Tubby struggled with his nine-times table
   and whispered a rude joke to Sniffy Snape,
   until the headmaster walked in, spoke softly
   to Miss Banks, and we all stood up.

Peter Holliday, January 2018.

NO STOCKING

Father Christmas never visited me.
No! He never visited me.
I never had a stocking or even a sock.
No! I never had a stocking.

You see I was an orphan.
My aunt in service took me in.
You see I was only five.
My life was to be in service.
I was only five.

Christmases came, Christmases went.
The servants busy with festivities.
Christmases came, Christmases went.
I was given a penny,
a new set of clothes for the next year.
No! I never had a stocking.

Eighty years later
I stayed with friends for Christmas.
Father Christmas came to their house.
I had my first stocking ever.
What a joy to feel those mysterious shapes!
I was overcome.

Bryony Cullum.
A true story about a friend of my mother's, Elsie.

UNTIL WE MEET AGAIN

The time has come for me to say farewell –
I hope I may have cast the tiniest spell
on opening up your eyes so very wide
to the wonders of our lovely countryside.

For wherever I have steered my pen –
from the babbling brook to a Highland glen,
from the otter's holt to the raven's nest –
in the Radnor hills we have been a guest.
So remember this birthright is always yours –
both purple heather and yellow gorse –
just keep it safe for those that follow on,
so they too will respect it when we're gone.

Now, hopefully on one bitter winter's night
I shall take up my pen and again start to write;
For I still have so many stories yet to tell.
It's goodbye from me for now – I wish you well.

John Elmes.

THOMAS FRANCIS JAMES KINOULTY 1915-1994

The poem that follows is about my dad, who was born in Ireland at the time of great political unrest, leading up to the Civil War and the establishment of The Irish Free State in 1922. His father, an Irish speaking Catholic, was a sergeant in the Royal Irish Constabulary, which made him an automatic target for the IRA. The RIC was disbanded in 1922 and many were resettled elsewhere. My dad's family was resettled in Coventry when he was 8 years old.

Thomas Francis James Kinoulty – an honest, brave and upright man,
hewn from the rock of County Clare, home of the Kinoulty clan.
Early childhood, civil war; rumours, fear and threat abound,
rifles firing, soldiers shouting – all became a common sound.
The family fled in terror and next called Coventry home,
a long way from Mount Callan and the waves with crashing foam.

Thomas Francis James Kinoulty – a loyal, reserved and generous man,
shy and awkward in school photos, two left feet and two left hands.
Gifted elder brother, going on to be a priest
died at 19 of pneumonia, his mother's joy forever ceased.
Long nights spent in study, occupied with law,
called to serve his country at the outbreak of war.

Thomas Francis James Kinoulty – a kind and selfless, caring man,
married late my Irish mother, a happy family life began.
Local government in Sussex, babies born to happy days,
living life with simple, traditional Irish ways.
He played and walked, picked blackberries, read story books aloud,
passed on his love of poetry, did William Shakespeare proud.

Thomas Francis James Kinoulty lacked some ordinary skills;
no DIY nor gardening, no culinary thrills.
He never mastered driving, we walked a lot instead,
playing games of "A for Apple" – I still do it in my head.
A lifelong love of learning, an interest in the news,
adventurous foreign travel, conservative Catholic views.

Thomas Francis James Kinoulty, things I never will forget:
farmers' hands and snow white hair – the kindest man I ever met.
Boswell's Life of Johnson, Jane Austen by his side,
his family's achievements a source of constant pride.

Life wasn't always easy, he struggled with his weight,
had the remnants of a stammer and more than one OCD trait,
but with generosity and humour and unassuming ways
he lived his life with courage to the ending of his days.

Dorothy Kennedy.

UNCLE BERT

My uncle Bert knew exactly
the length of any particular piece of string;
that 'how high' was a Chinaman;
and how many beans made five.

He cracked each finger knuckle one by one
until I winced, and played a waltz or '1812'
by tapping a ruler on his teeth.

His head shone bright as the morning sun
as he juggled apples in the kitchen
or spun a glittering plate across the table.

A croak that made the dozing frog look up;
a whistle that prompted the blackbird to reply,
and brought him curious to the damson tree;
a laugh that startled the baby in his pram;
a belch that disgusted my mother and angered my aunt –
no wonder I waited all summer
for the blast of his horn and the over-revved engine.

So one hot August, when for once he had
failed to whirl in, on the day I had marked in red
on my 'Beano' calendar, I grew concerned...

Father's face was tight, and white with rage:
"Bert won't be coming to this house again.
he's buggered off to Spain with the girl next door!"

How quickly weather changes – then began
months of thick cloud, years of sharp rain.

Peter Holliday.

AUNT ELSIE

No mistaking her surely –
as tall as my aunt Elsie,
long, lugubrious face;
fag hanging from her lower lip;
thin as the flagpole in the square.

Here she comes blaspheming
like Saul or Caiaphas;
gin before breakfast, brandy after it;
slapping and barging her way
through what's left of her life.

A pity, don't you think?
Well, I do anyway, knowing
the crap hand circumstance

has dealt her: husband
an invalid, ex-miner.

Coughing his heart out on a cold mattress;
coal-dust silting up his lungs;
one shoulder higher than the other
where a sharp slab struck him
and laid him out for years.

Grim terraces shadowed by the slag heap;
shared bog-hole; one water-pump
between sixteen; ten-foot yard
to hang the washing, scrub and shout –
just enough room to spit in.

Small wonder she thrashed her children.
One was toughened by it, growing
to be a quick strong boy; the other
waned, a frail unhappy girl
who couldn't think or speak. She died.

It's not my aunt, of course. She
gave up the struggle years ago
and was burnt to a tiny jar of ash –
but I cross and turn and watch her
as she strides off down the street.

Peter Holliday.

RIDE A PAINTED PONY

Childhood memories of life on a farm in the fifties at Hop Picking.

Ride a painted pony, a line from a long forgotten song.
Pictures from my childhood flash into my mind.

Can I put the pony in the paddock, mister?
My father, whose heart was as big as his frame, would say, "Yes".

The Romanies were here again for hop picking.
One hundred or more,
with their gaily lined tents.

The ponies in the paddock would come and go silently in the night.
Often thirty, forty, fifty, who knows?

In the morning we would eagerly look out of the window.
The paddock was empty not a painted pony in sight.

The favour returned, the gypsy women
patrolled the house,
keeping mother, my sister and me safe.

Father could sneak out, up the long drive,
to run his beloved football team.

Margaret Dallow.

Many years ago on the island of Bute, the 'Women's Rural' was one of the few organisations women could attend away from the demands of rural life. They sometimes walked miles through the bracken to attend their monthly meetings, where they could chat together, share recipes and compare handcrafts. But most importantly they could take part in the competitions set for each meeting. The following poem captures the life of a widow, excitedly preparing a 'clootie dumplin' for a competition that very evening.

A GRAND NICHT OOT

We're well in tae anither year
and February is nearly here.
There's been a lot o' frost and snaw
but ma banes forecast, there'll be a thaw.

It's aye the same this time o' year,
there's very little unco' cheer.
But patiently a sit an wait,
for the sound o' the latch, at my frontgate.

A sit alane at my fireside,
an think o' Wullie wi' great pride.
The doctor could'na mak him better,
and noo he's wae our Bless'd Maker.

The neebours aye pop in tae look,
a hardly even need to cook,
in they come wi bowls o' broth,
that wid dae justice tae a toff.

But our dear Lord's been guid tae me,
there's naethin a want, that I can see.

The weans a' just seem to prosper,
wans even noo become a doctor.

Thankfully I hae food in ma belly,
an the weans hae even gien me a telly.
A can gang tae bed when am feeling drowsy,
snug in something ca'd a downie.

But it's Monday, an I'm no jist sitting aboot,
for this is the nicht that I go oot.
There's a competeetition on the nicht,
an a've set tae work wi a' ma micht.

In ma old een, there's a wee bit glimmer,
the pot's on the fire, just set tae simmer,
I'm sure my dumplin will win the approval,
o' the judges at the Ballianlay Rural.

Moyra Taylor.

CHILDREN'S POETRY

Winning poems from the March 2018 Children's Poetry Competition

MY FAVOURITE TIME OF THE YEAR

The snowflakes shimmering on the horizon beyond the hills;
The winter has arrived.
Crackling leaves we find on the drive.
We search for our warmest clothes,
Our woolliest jumpers at the bottom of our drawers.
Squirrels running from park to park,
Looking for acorns to bury and
Hedgehogs hibernating in clumps of leaves.

The winter is over.
The sun has come out.

Bronya Lewis. Age 7.

Written at her grandmother's as a spontaneous decision. Pupil at Ashperton School.

FIREWORKS

Bing, Bang, Bash, Boom
Fireworks shooting up to the sky
Spreading in the blank canvas
Popping and puffing
The fireworks are rainbow glazed.
Fireworks yelling as they fly up into the sky
Slowly, falling down to the ground
Like a dragon's sneeze
Gently dying on the ground.

Lilit Martirossian. Age 8.

Stoke Prior School.

A POEM OF WAR

Bang, grenades being thrown, bombs being dropped,
Dog fights in the sky, men flying down on their parachutes
Fighting for their country
Praying for victory.

People hiding in the Anderson Shelters
Hoping that their homes are not destroyed.
Mothers and children pack their bags
Evacuating to the countryside.

Food supplies are low.
Ration books are handed out.
The men are all at war,
The women working the land.

Eleven eleven the fighting stopped.
Guns dropped and bodies lay fallen.

Silence swept across the land.
Poppies began to grow in Flander's fields.

Harry Dallow.
Year 5, Wigmore Primary School.

POVERTY

All the food left on our plates taken for granted,
All the clothes and toys we cry about
Because its not the one you wanted.
All the money wasted on expensive cars,
Not caring about the victims living through violent wars
Constantly hearing: BANG...BANG... BANG.

Adverts pleading for your help,
And hearing skinny and hungry dogs yelp.
Children crying for their late parents
Stuck in a pile of rubble,
And vulnerable youths trying to smuggle food
Into their empty pockets.

Newborns on the verge of death,
Taking in each weak breath.

Families dragging bottles of contaminated water,
Not knowing that each sip could kill a son or daughter.

Kate Weaver. Age 12.
Queen Elizabeth High School, Bromyard.

WHEN...

When... we went on the dunes.
February,
An exciting, a chilled, a comical, a fun filled week
In Lanzarote,
A sandy, a bustling, a windy, a hustling country.
The sun shone like a lantern, as if it were a dream
So therefore mum had to lather me from head to toe in sun cream.
In the rental car we zoomed away,
Because we were going out for the day.
The destination approached and a bumpy landscape lay out before me,
And ten bumpy animals were spitting and stomping, who smelled a bit like wee.
They lay, all down and I climbed in the chair over his hump.
A tall man somehow told him to stand up and it all happened with a crash and a bump.
The name of this creature was a camel, and a camel is a large hairy mammal.
Slowly we started to trek up the sand dunes, whilst holding on for dear life,
And I guess you could say that doing this activity put my mum and I at strife.
Five minutes in, the sky was swallowed in darkness and the sun went away,
Drops of water splattered on my head each one quicker than the other,
The rain was definitely here to stay...
In the blink of an eye, the dunes went apocalyptic, sand spiralling around and around,
The rain turned into unfathomable chunks of hail,
thumping down so hard you couldn't hear a sound.
The wind stole our sunglasses, hair bands and vision,
So the camels started going back down the dunes, it was a very mutual decision.
The storm calmed itself down and the raging winds flew off far,
With beaten up bodies because of the hail, we all wanted to go back to the villa,
So we clambered back in our car.

Isla Bayliss.
Year 9, Queen Elizabeth High School, Bromyard.

THE NATURAL WORLD

THE DUNNOCK

Here is the small, shy dunnock –
petite housewife of the hedgerow –
who has crept all winter
in the cold shadows
where cracked twigs, stiff roots, dead leaves
blow awkwardly together.

Now she has come out
into the February sun
and turns her pale breast
to the warmth
and shakes herself awake
and preens on a low branch.

She has made a neat nest
in the heart of the bush
and begins to line it
with down and moss and a little dry grass
as an act of endurance,
a gesture of hope.

Perhaps she dreams her unborn son
will be an eagle – golden, bold –
but knows, in her soul, these grey realities:
a tight and bounded corridor of thorns
broken in spring by tentative song
with glimpses of the wide sky overhead.

Peter Holliday, February 2016.

BIRD SONG

In the wood I was walking
when a single bird started singing
as the sun peeped between the trees.
A thunderstorm had just ended and
the fir trees smelt like fresh lemons
wafting on the breeze.

Suddenly the little bird was joined
by a chorus of many others
sitting in trees and briar bushes.
The air alive with music as their
trilling rose above them
filling every hidden corner
rising halfway to Heaven
pure
like angels on the wing.

All at once I was transported to a
vast cathedral with glass windows
casting shadows towards the sky
with the choir's sweet voices
cascading like running water
for my delight.
I listened to their song as I
drifted on and on, my low spirits lifting
up and up soaring with
God on high.

The birds sang for many hours
like it was the last day of the world
and they were singing, singing their
long goodbye.

Jane Dallow.

ON SHIPMAN HEAD DOWN

Through purple and green on the hill
runs the water in trickle and rill;
the grey clouds are past,
and the sun shines at last
bringing colour and life
after elements' strife.

Walking upwards on erica's spring,
watching bees moving low on the wing,
till I come to the top
and in wonderment stop –
to review ev'ry cloud,
and to ponder aloud:

At what height, and how fast, and from where
come these mountains and castles of air?
And the wide, rolling sea
ever rushes to be
on the rugged rocks wrecked –
all its power now checked.

Strong wind's bluster and freedom and pow'r
make complete this triumvirate's hour;
but the shine of the sun
invites all to have fun,
and the battle just fought
is for nought!

John Pare, summer 1985.

SEA GULLS IN THE SNOW

As I looked out from the window, I saw
the sea gulls in the snow,
floating, wheeling, sighing competing with the flakes.
Soaring and dropping, being enveloped in whiteness
the whistling wind all around, with Nature's combinations,
white and more pure white, only their black caps being significant,
unnatural surroundings for a bird of the sea.
Ghostly figures in a landscape, almost figments of the imagination
and still they circle minute after minute
what ceaseless motion, just a gentle flap of the wings
again and slowly again, timeless and tireless.
As the trillioned flakes slowly peter out the illusion is broken
they cannot compete with the stark naked atmosphere,
flying away to dance and play in other snows.

Mary Wakefield-Jones.

MOUNTAINS

Standing tall, above us all,
those giants on earth watch proud and still.
Reaching, reaching to the sky,
where only eagles dare to fly.

They hold their own secrets, none can reply,
yet the winds taunt these primaeval mountains,
whispering, whispering, "Tell us all",
but only the silence of these solemn giants is heard.
Sentinels they watch all below,
the sun and moon lighting the way.
Unmoved by lightning, rain, fiery floods,
as snow and ice engulf the ravines and crevasses in their lonely exile.

Below in fields, lakes and forests,
they watch as humans toil for life,
obeying the seasons as they come,
the unremitting times – but they survive it all.

What stories could they tell us,
of man's struggle of life and joy,
when race follows race, and man flies ahead,
into eternal bliss yet still unknown.
The solemn sounds are enfolded,
deep within their solitude.
No man may know the secrets that they hold,
as innocently they keep their watch until we are no more.

Moyra Taylor, 2016.

WHERE ARE THE BEES?

How quiet is the Hive,
where are the Bees?
Are they dead?

Wait with baited breath
where are the Bees?
Have they fled?

How will the world be fed?
Cherry ripe, apples, pears,
pink blossom
waiting for pollination.

Farmer's crops, wild hedgerows
roses in the Old Churchyard.
Lilies in the pond,
wild heather on the moors.

Waiting for the bees to come.
are they playing Hide and Seek?

Everything is quiet
listening, waiting for the
sound of buzzing
when the Bees start swarming.

Where are the Bees?
Are they sleeping?

There is a stillness
an expectation,
where are the Bees?
Queen, drones, workers
full of nectar
will there be honey
to spread with butter?

Jane Dallow.

THREE GARDENS

The best thing in my garden
is the pear tree that I climb,
and the hedge that I hide inside,
my castle and my den.
I like the bed of lupins
where my cat goes to sleep,

and I love my mother's roses
because they smell so sweet.

We had to make the garden,
digging beds for flowers and veg;
we took out leylandii
and planted a beech hedge.
We moved the lawn, which was quite steep,
planting shrubs and sowing seeds,
fourteen kinds of veg we grew to eat,
composting each year, my goodness, what a treat!

Now no more a lawn to mow,
no more a hedge to cut,
we sit in the sun to contemplate
the warm brick walls and gravel path.
But lo! A blaze of violets now bestrew,
a gravel path no more;
and crocus, cyclamen in spring
all have come anew.

For we can't help still sowing seed
and planting this and that;
hanging baskets – buckets – pots –
it matters not a lot.
Our hearts are in our garden,
it gives us daily pleasure;
we fight the bugs – especially slugs –
and thus defend our treasure.

Thalia Gordon Clark.

TREES
A Personal View

Potential pencils and pads of paper
march in serried ranks towards the dawn.
Light lingering on leaves
and fine filtered fingers,
a golden glow on burning bright branches
-burning...

looking to a future of black picture sticks
created for creating
thro' smudges, sweeps of black on white
a representation of ...
potential pencils.

Maggie McGladdery.

CROW

The loud rude crow
skims the tiles of the house,
blocking the sun for a moment,
casting a black shadow.

Bully-boy, road-hog, lout –
hoodie, with the hood pulled up
so's we can't identify him –
he's first to the waste-bin and the dung-yard.

He hangs round abattoirs and battlefields
looking for livers and eyeballs,
and tears gobbets of offal from the road –
the corpses of things we care nothing about.

He knows we ought to reward him –
surly waiter, clearing up the mess we've made...
if beaks could grin he'd grin –
and I've seen him wink and chuckle.

He thinks he owns the earth
and I'm not sure he doesn't.

Peter Holliday, June 2011.

STRAWBERRIES

Your hair is what they call Strawberry Blonde,
I know that now,
golden freckles across
your upturned nose.

We fed one another strawberries
from the plants upon the ground,
each one red and juicy
delicious to behold.

The day was hot and drowsy
the humming of the honey bees
was the only sound that carried
on the summer-scented breeze.

So I stole a kiss
from your strawberry tasting lips.
You smiled your strawberry smile and
the strawberry juice from lip to lip
mingled for a while.

I remember every detail of that day
how I stole a kiss from your strawberry-tasting lips
when we were ten years old.

Jane Dallow.

MY GARDEN

What is this space I call my garden?
Does the grass know I own it?
Do the flowers watch me?
Do they love me for the care I give? –
I have no answer.

Are the lilacs giving me their scent?
Daffodils looking down
golden and yellow frills all shy.

Can I be a moving flower?
Surrounded by my beautiful friends
sharing their innocent world.

Judy Malet.

THE SEA

In the beginning, the alpha,
here was light and darkness, when matter filled space,
and waters, like growing pains, converged
crashing together, controlled by some esoteric force
that sculptured the unknown, creating me,
I am – the Sea.

I surround you, yet never still, listening
as I keep a watchful eye on all that I behold,
and it was then, in that first flux of embryonic chaos
that life began – evolution – and then man.

From that astral primordial dawn,
watching Odysseus build his Homeric ship.
Bestilled, veiled in a space of silence, tentatively waiting,
until through my portal, Odysseus eloped from the clutches of Calypso.

Gentle winds caressed the blue-white silken sails,
piloting him across my sea,
towards unforetold chapters.
Zeus' storms overwhelmed unbeknown waters,
navigating Odysseus through many vulnerable voyages,
rescuing his seduced sailors from the grip of the sucking Lotus Eaters,
and their intoxicating lotus plant.

Heroically battling foul play, into the vacuous unforeseen,
propelled by blind forces towards the dreaded Cyclops and Sirens,
until Odysseus and his men, were unshackled and delivered safely.
I am the Sea – I was there.

And so too, on that umbracious evening,
when all around was calm,
and only my soft monotonous cadence
mingled with the voices of His men,
unquestioningly, keeping faith with His commands,
setting sail for Genneseret.
But soon the silver winged breeze
was awakened by cataclysmic single-mindedness,
whence from calm, I was forced to become a youlin sea,
as wind and rain relentlessly stabbed the men like a whetted knife.
They, grappling with fear, grabbing empty spaces,
faith faltering, foundering, spiralling,
until a faint ghost-like figure appeared
walking towards them, treading the waves.
Clear sight was suffocated by murky fog and squalls.
Suddenly, through a vent,
a dart of moonlight broke through,
sufficing to make the phantom figure recognisable – it was Him.

Through power and grace,
the winds and rain obeyed His commands,
both elements and men, descending into a mesmerising calm –
He was once more with them.
I was witness to this, at Galilee.
I am the Sea, I was there.

Later in the vale of perpetuity,
Eriksson upped anchor in Greenland searching for new lands westwards.
In buffeting winds over a timeless sea, set off-course,
driven fortuitously towards uncharted land,
the fabled New World came into sight – Vinland.

Columbus too ventured forth from Portugal,
seeking a westward passage to the Orient,
guided only by the light of the sun;
the elusive destination remained faceless,
until he reached terra firma – the Bahamas – San Salvador.
I am the Sea, and I was there.

Now, I playfully frolic with the sands,
where my frothy waves draw the pebbles
back and forth along the fringe.
A soft, unrhymed lyrical line.
Seagulls cry, gliding through uninterrupted azure skies –
"Awake! Awake!" – dawn cannot be delayed,
it is time – and once again man appears.
It is a new day, and I am waiting, watching, listening.
I am the Sea, and I am here.

Moyra Taylor, 2016.

HUMOUR

MADUSHA REST

This is a Guest House at Maskeliya, Sri Lanka in which my second son, his family and teaching staff had to live for the better part of a year. I only stayed there for a couple of weeks! Hamantha is the owner.

Madusha Rest, Madusha Rest
is run by something of a pest:
he scrimps and saves at ev'ry turn –
it seems, somehow, he cannot learn
that doing something well, just once,
results in being less a dunce
than doing something many times
with poor materials, saving dimes.

Madusha Rest, Madusha Rest,
is not for the discerning guest:
the rain seeps in; the paintwork's thin;
it seems the landlord's never in
to deal with problems as they come,
and when he's there it's like you're dumb
(or he is deaf) for he'll just do
small parts of what you want him to.

Madusha Rest, Madusha Rest,
one cannot speak of it with zest.
The water (when there is) is cold,
unless one pays more, one is told.
"You want a towel, sir, you must
be joking"; you say, "But it's just!"
Hamantha: "That's an extra cost,
or all my profit will be lost."

Madusha Rest, Madusha Rest,
you ought to see it one time, lest

you think that I exaggerate,
and that it's really, really great.
You may go near, you may go far,
it's really only worth one star;
from north to south, from east to west,
there's only one Madusha Rest.
(Thank God!)

John Pare, December, 2011.

THE SQUIRREL AND THE CLEANER

There was a squirrel
Always in a whirrel
and a house cleaner
who couldn't be meaner!

She said to the squirrel
I could use your taily whirrel!
Oh, said the squirrel
for a nut or two
what can I do?

The cobwebs and cobwebs
with a tail like yours
and those clever paws
you could whirl them away
could be done everyday!

Judy Malet.

MY SHADOW

Look at my shadow on the wall
first it's big and now it's small;
put the light out
it's not there at all.

Mary Wakefield-Jones.

SIX STARLINGS

Six starlings screech in, like boys on motorbikes,
and skid to a halt on the lawn.
They're high on maggots and leatherjackets,
shoving each other aside,
chaffing and scrapping, sharp beaks
stabbing the scrubby turf,
showing off to their girlfriends.

Hold on! They're zooming off
to bully the bird-table,
squirting the fence with white stuff,
shouting: "Clean it up, sucker!"

Hear them each night in the hawthorns
burping, swapping exploits and dirty jokes,
snorting into the small hours.

We 'tut-tut' and draw the curtain tight.
"This used to be a respectable neighbourhood!"

Peter Holliday.

BUS FROM NELSON'S DOCKYARD

Late afternoon
tired, hot.
History absorbed.

Bus full returning locals.
Politeness
no automatic door.
The passenger nearest
their duty to close.
Air conditioning off
saves on petrol the passengers tell us.

Very different passenger
held in a plastic bag.
Its head out watching all around.
A very large Turtle.
Its possessor pats it gently.
My friend whispers "It must be a pet!"
I smile but my thoughts are of supper and a pot!

Rosemarie J. Powell, winter 2012-2013.

GNATzzzzzz

Small flappers
flapping
and wing tips
tapping.
A Tiny Gnat
napping
on a hot summer's day
Bzzzz
zzz

z

A short tail
tipping
and sweet lips
sipping.
A nasty Gnat
nipping
on a late summer's day.
Bzzzz
zzz

z

Mary Wakefield-Jones.

CONCEALING AND REVEALING

Concealing and revealing is the way with certain cats
who go out in the countryside and bring home little rats.
They fertle in the dense hedgerows until they find the nest,
then pounce and paw and petrify until they have the best.
Then they meander homewards with rat that dangles down
and do not once anticipate their human's angry frown!

Once in thro' cat flap, yowl begins to announce their gruesome find.
They think the people will be thrilled and that their gift is kind!

But now concealing is the game and soon the prey is hid
behind the chair or under rug as if to make a lid!
Reveal is not the greatest thing for anyone to do,
when cat's forgotten treasured rat – and it has turned to goo!!

Maggie McGladdery.

SHORT POEMS AND HAIKUS

A haiku is a Japanese poem of 17 syllables; 3 lines of 5,7, 5 syllables

FOUR VARIATIONS ON 'LITTLE MISS MUFFET';

The Spider

"I'm very fond of whey", said the spider rather sadly,
it's very hard to come by, and I miss it rather badly;
I'm not so keen on curds, although they sometimes take my fancy,
and yesterday I saw some in a bowl inscribed with 'Nancy'."

"Nancy Muffet was her name, as I've heard a rumour tell it;
her father sees a chestnut tree and then proceeds to fell it.
He chops it up and makes a frame, and then begins to stuff it;
he gives it to his girl to test, and sells it as 'a tuffet'."

"She sat on one just yesterday, and clutched her little bowlful;
I hadn't had a meal for days, and felt a little soulful.
I didn't mean to frighten her so she would go and drop it –
her tummy just looked over-full, and whey might go and pop it!"

"The silly girl, she leapt so high (perhaps I dropped too quickly?);
she came to earth and stood there looking just a little sickly!
She ran away, the curds and whey slipped slowly down the tuffet;
I may as well resign myself: for weeks more I must rough it."

Mr Muffet
(To be sung to the tune to "Christians awake! Salute the happy morn")

Muffet's my name, a carpenter by trade;
live with my daughter in a woody glade.
This teems with wildlife, and I love it all;
my daughter likes the big ones, not the small.
Today I found her – my hat, what a mess!
a spider'd poured whey over all her dress!

A Neighbouring Mouse

I am a mouse,
my little house
is rather prone to flooding.
The other day
there came my way
the product of cows' cudding.

A milk bath's fine,
and also wine –
I must confess I like them;

water's for me,
though not the sea;
minnow's that pass, I spike them.

It's just too much –
though curds as such
I like because they're cheesy –
when through my door
and o'er my floor
comes whey – it makes me sneezy!

Miss Muffet

I love curds and whey, I do –
I eat them all the time.
I never get enough of them
and Blow me! what a crime:

I sat there all serene and good –
my spoon was poised above –
then spinning down above my head
a spider came and wove

a web above my bowl – he did,
I tell the honest truth!
I jumped up, shrieked and ran like mad –
he startled me, forsooth.

He didn't get it though – I made
quite sure that it was spilt.
I'll have to go and wake the cow
(moos with an Irish lilt!).

John Pare, c.1970.

UNTITLED

What is love
through our lives?
Sometimes it dances by;
We can never know
because love can be shy.
But if it's really mine
will it hide behind
a Valentine!!!

Judy Malet.

THE POET

He touches the soul in me
giving me a hungered peace
and a pleasure so deep.
Like finding gold or diamonds that glint,
wrought from the birth of this God-made earth.
He opens the door
and I walk through.

Josie Ann Dolan.

HEDGEHOG/HOGLET

Oh dear! There you are again,
little prickly lurches
as you sniffle through the leaves –
you're a hoglet lost and looking
for a winter home
but you don't hang up your coat and
wander in.
Oh dear! Should I open the door and
offer you a leafy bed?

YES!

Judy Malet.

FOUR HAIKUS

COLD NIGHT

The white, hoar-bright grass
sparkles under my torch-beam
beneath scattered stars.

SUNRISE

You came to my life
like a slow-growing sunrise –
changed it for ever!

MORNING LIGHT

Out of a cleft cloud
some celestial searchlights
enlighten the hills.

CLOUDS

A cloud flotilla,
charcoal against duck-egg blue,
sails the ev'ning sky.

John Pare.

A GIFT FROM THE SEA

Down on the beach
I saw it far away
I watched the shiny curve.
I waited on the golden sand,
it began to break.
Silver glitter
it scattered around my feet
the gift of a wave.

Judy Malet.

ABROAD

EXPLORERS AND TRAVELLERS

No, we are not explorers; just have been
to strange lands, singly or together, seen
the oldest building in the shaft sunk down
at Jericho; admired from Christchurch town
the Southern Alps snow-tipped across the plain;
travelled right down to Sicily by train;
watched the waved albatrosses leave the cliff;
admired the so-clearly-chiselled hieroglyph –
seen Papuan warriors loping to revenge
an insult to their folk; walked round Stonehenge –

And yet our most adventurous move till now
was coming up to live near sheep and cow,
forest and farm, though London born, and bred
in Surrey, choosing country life instead
of parish duties and a sober round
of worthy life, till safely under ground.
But one more change has now come to explore
and see if fate has yet new things in store –
town life will surely not be all that bad
(I'd quite forgot; we're off to Trinidad!)

Charles Gordon Clark.

JOURNEY TO HALF MOON BAY, ANTIGUA

To St. John's
find the Bus Station
for the west-side island destination.
Internet directions:
walk north on Market;
at first Stop sign
turn right on High Street.
Hustle and bustle, many buses,
no markers here for route destinations.

"To Half Moon Bay?" I enquire;
driver says, "Yes, this one."
Lesson learned not to board too early –
driver will not leave till bus is full.

I look around:
a long way to equality –
no women drivers here.

Looking out to see the island
it shows a diverse landscape:
industrial, and little wooden houses,
most brightly painted shining in the sun.
But many in need of repair.
As we travel through the centre
of the island, some cultivation –
this land drained of its soil-goodness;
the island has been used for growing sugar –
a dark and uneasy past.

A herd of sad-looking cattle, no Herefords here;
goats tethered grazing on the scrub land.

Antiguan passenger – a commentary for my pleasure; politeness abounds:
Half Moon Bay – the bus will take you there, but not
his regular route – extra dollars to pay, though just a few.

The Bay opens up before us as we descend, true to its name.
Driver says, "Will be back by three."

No Beach Hawkers here like Castaway;
just Denny's Bar under the mangoes, and a table of local craft.

We walk the beach shade found by mango trees.
Turquoise lagoon to swim.
The only sound, waves crashing on the rocks surrounding the lagoon;
spray over six feet; wild, gentle, calm.

We climb to look out across the aquamarine ocean,
sails billowing, boats' destination may be South America?

Returning to the shade
a brightly coloured bird in the tree,
it's song pretty, but so thin in sound.

Rosemarie J. Powell.

JOURNEY HOME FROM HALF MOON BAY

We were there at three – no bus in sight.
We were asked, "Would you like a lift
to the designated bus stop
three miles up the hill?"
Kindness and politeness on this island abounds.

We sit in a lonely bus shelter –
provided by the community, it says.
Our new friend waits with us.
She came from New Guinea
fifteen years ago.
A better life,
raising her son.
To college he will go.
She commutes every day eight miles on the bus
to her job in Half Moon Bay.

Rosemarie J. Powell.

Half Moon Bay is protected – Part of Antigua Island National Park.
May it so remain!

SRI LANKAN BEAUTY

The placid waters of the reservoir
reflect the tea-bush-covered hills tonight.
They echo homestead light and moving car
beneath a part-starred sky, and all seems right.

But … should we look to earlier days, what then?
Was there a village where the lake now lies?
Who its inhabitants, who felt what, when
the moving order came: "The waters rise!"?

The tea plantations, with the colours bright
of women's sarees dotted 'cross the hill,
make tourist picture postcards look just right;
the sunshine-smiles speak to us of goodwill.

But … venture from your western lodge to view
the line rooms where they spend th'exhausted hours,
once they have worked a twelve-hour shift, and you
might wonder at their paupers' lives 'gainst yours.

The railway snakes 'cross countryside steep-hilled,
affording views spectacular and base.
The light shines on the curving lines; is killed
by tunnel, or by high trees' shad'wing lace.

But … how (by whom?) was access slowly gained?
Who dug the cuttings, piled the earth up high
where vales required embankments? Men retained
for pence by Brits who sought rich trade to ply.

The little man still suffers to this day –

the main resource in countries near and far –
with little voice with which to have his say.
He suffers too when leaders wage cruel war.

We use 'man' for the populace, but hide
beneath this term the plight of women too,
so often more repressed, kept down, denied
full rights, without a single pers'nal sou.

Why is it difficult for all to see
the equal worth that ev'ry person has?
Is fear, and greed for pow'r, what seem to be
the cause, and make the few suppress the mass?

John Pare, November 2009.

HISTORY – WAR

MIST

It was on a June night, in marshy ground near a burn,
below the crags of a castle besieged by the English,
that the eerie mist bestowed a story
told by many, resounding throughout the kingdom.

Our King Robert waited patiently,
waiting for the curtain of mist to rise,
before attacking the great English Army
whose numbers far outweighed his own.

Edward's armed soldiers stood proud,
reinforced by yet more men –
men with longbows at the ready –
listening to Scots' voices whispering through the mist.

Robert's men waited patiently, undeterred by numbers,
standing knee-deep in mist,
not burdened by armour, but light-footed,
in plaids – sticks gripped ready to hammer Edward's army.

Throughout the night the Scottish King paced up and down,
tendrils of mist dancing to and fro,
until a long-awaited gap appeared, and they attacked,
those brave few, resolute, determined, full of mettle.

The first war of independence had begun,
a landmark in the history of Scotland;
in this floating mist King Robert The Bruce won the day –
the year was 1314, and this was the Battle of Bannockburn.

Moyra Taylor.

GREEN MAN CARVING

Just a piece of wood
Years of branches and leaves

The buds of spring
the richness of summer
the gold of autumn
the bareness of winter

Now I delve with the sharpness of man-made tools
create and discover
the grains and patterns

The challenge is keeping
and sharing it all
as the Green Man appears.

Judy Malet.

THE MISTS OF MEMORY AND THOUGHTFULNESS

Down the winding pot-holed road of memory, half hidden in the mists of time,
nuggets of happiness, sadness, fears and tears drift through the
mountains we tried to climb;
back in the Thirties the grown-ups talked of nothing but war –
the mists of time not yet hidden the horrors of the one before.
To the country's call dads and sons, brothers and lovers left to fight in
lands across the sea;

111

old men, wives and children now had to take the places where these
heroes used to be.
Our country school doubled in size as we received ashen-faced children
fleeing from hell,
now standing in line with us country kids at the sound of the old school bell.

Every Sunday morning, and sometimes after work, my dad would don
his Home Guard kit
with three stripes on his sleeve and medal-ribbons on his chest, willing
to do his bit.
Military conflict was no stranger to him; at 17 he left the farm and took
the King's shilling;
four years on, a trained soldier in the K.S.L.I., and the First World War
was just beginning.
Then followed Ypres, the Somme barbed wire, shells, mud, gas and the
Military Medal and Bar;
but he survived, and these horrific memories he wrapped and hid in
the mists of time.

Now the war that the grown-ups talked about was made real with gas-
masks and the blackout;
his two sons, my brothers, donned uniforms of Air-Force blue and
went off to fight.
For months on end no news was heard, and we all hoped they were both alright.

All we knew was that one was on the Southern coast operating a Bofors gun,
working with a searchlight battery in order to shoot down the dreaded Hun;
the other being a despatch rider, guiding convoys from airfields in
some foreign land,
taking provisions and mail from home to the lads of the fighting band.

To me and my family God was kind: my father and brothers and all we
held dear
lived happily on for many years, in a land of plenty without any fear.

These memories are treasures
not in a chest with a lock of gold
but wrapped in the mists of memory,
and will probably never be told.

Denis R.H. Teal.

BURMA STARS

Men far from home and hearth,
toiled long through steaming green
hacking down its tangled web,
the viper coiled unseen.

Sweat evaporating beneath an unforgiving sun
the whip hand, across their burning flesh.
Each man becoming half himself,
shovelling, shallow graves with every sleeper laid.
Each brave heart a rising epitaph.

Josie Ann Dolan.

A QUESTION OF WAR

Let us remember the First and Second World Wars
where so many were left emotionally poor
when will the world celebrate
the last of all wars?

Judy Malet.

RELIGIOUS, PHILOSOPHICAL, MISCELLANEOUS

ARE YOU RELIGIOUS?

Are you religious? I don't know what you mean.
Would it involve a church or mosque?
Attending a service or ringing bells?
Are you thinking of candles or wearing black?
Or silence or chanting for hours and hours?

I don't want a creed, but I do want a journey
to draw from that ocean of love;
so if you mean touching the depths of myself,
finding the music, seeing the colour,
if you mean drawing in love from life,
then I hope I am, I hope I am.

If you mean finding I'm one with the hills,
one with the trees and the bees and the seas;
if you mean understanding and smiling –
then I hope I am, I hope I am.

Thalia Gordon Clark.

THE DARKNESS CRUMBLES

Darkness like thunder clouds intensifying
like black smog, drifting, enclosing, suffocating.
We writhe in nightmare constricting bed clothes
heart pounding, sweating.
Dark thoughts slither subterraneously.

What can break into the amorphous mass
to cause it to crumble like grain in a silo,
like cliffs into the sea?

We do not know what may happen next,
a chance snippet of conversation,
a snatch of newsprint,
a physical disruption
may give a clue,
could we say hope is born?
A hand is being held out.

One day, we believe it might happen;
the darkness could crumble.
Suddenly or stealthily the pressure lessens,
we can expand, explore, see visions.
The fortified darkness has cracked, crumbled, dispersed.
We are free!.

Bryony Cullum.

A hope to move away from depression

BLOW THE COACH HORN

A stagecoach driver by the name of Fate
with four-in-hand at the starting gate,
taking a group of folk to a land called The Future –
a destination never visited before –
steeds that go by the names of Laughter, Hope, Smiles, and Tears
will travel through hamlets called Beauty, Hope, and Fears,
villages and towns full of smiles and frowns.

Through the large rear window is the highway of The Past,
by meadows and fields of broken promises so fast;
when they have crossed The River Of No Return
they will have reached that land called The Future
with no more bridges to burn,
no going forward, no going back –
this land called The Future is draped in black.

Denis R.H. Teal.

FERROUS EXHIBITION

(Inspired by an exhibition of artistic metalwork at the Hereford Museum)

The dance of change
delving around and through
creating anew
through heat and pressure
fresh treasure.

Here the silence, the space
to view the new
curated, creating a view
of solidity, hard, remembering the fire
when all was fluid
surrounded by passionate noise and spark,
inspired by softness,
manipulation, precision of mark,
love of process and inspiration.

Maggie McGladdery.

METALMORPHOSIS

For days I had heard roars, thumps, screeches,
suddenly I was exposed from thousands of years of compression,
discomfited, heated, changed from solid to liquid.

Nothing happened for quite a while
after I'd gained room temperature,
sliced apart and given a rectangular body.

Ooh! I am red hot! Being banged, stretched, curved and patterned.
What could I be? A bit of machinery, a tool?
I fancied seeing more of this space, this world.
Could my dream be realised?

I was aware of a furnace – bright, red, orange, fiery,
but also heavy breathing, a snorting close by me.

Something huge and moving – had it meaning for me?

Heated again, I felt an intimate connection,
smelt an odour of burnt hoof; I was moulded, nailed,
finally stood upon by a hairy, smelly monster.

The adventures began.
I clipped, clopped from stable to field,
to village and town, in event to event.
My host became famous.

I wore out! A devastating final separation!
To the scrap heap? No! I was placed
in the centre of the kitchen mantelpiece,
the heart of the family; what more could I want –
placed next to the photo of my champion Shire

Bryony Cullum.

Written in response to a workshop task-to write a poem from
the view point of an inanimate object.

A GOLDEN CHAIN OF EVENTS

It was just a discarded old log from a redundant woodpile
that had lain there for years, and been saved from the fire
hidden deep in the nettles; then I climbed o'er the stile
Where I managed to reach it, near some rusty barbed wire.

Its bark was discoloured, the seasons had bleached white

with one end split open and signs of rot and decay,
but I just knew as I took it out into the sunlight
that I'd found something special, while walking that day.

The next morning would find me down in my work shed
in the cold light of morning, wondering what I had found;
there I sawed off the rot, and on the lathe it was mounted;
I switched on the grindstone, and my lathe chisels found.

The sparks showered red as their cutting edge sharpened
with cold water dips, ensuring the temper was fine.
As the lathe started humming, an idea was fashioned
with the gouge resting on the tool rest, awaiting the sign.

As I started to turn it, with the lathe slowly revolving,
I turned into the sapwood as the bark peeled away:
the colour of coffee and with the chisel now singing,
as the ribbons of shavings flew past me that day.

The heartwood was golden, with dark chocolate patches
complementing the sapwood, of coffee and cream,
and it took on the shape of a most beautiful goblet,
as if another hand turned, and watched from a dream.

Finally it was finished, to be sanded quite lightly,
then sealed and polished, until it shone with a glow
to give endless pleasure, this thing of such beauty –
just a piece of old firewood, from long, long ago.

But what was this timber that gave all these qualities,
for it was not ash, oak, nor damson or yew.
Just a small garden tree, not a well-renowned species
but a piece of laburnum – Golden Chain to a few.

So now when I'm walking along country byways,
I hope for something special to perhaps catch my eye;
so that its beauty will shine through for always
and those ribbons of shavings will once again fly.

John Elmes, 1943-2017.

THE CREATOR

The mountains He made of rocky cregs,
the wetlands He covered with emerald green segs,
He made the rivers the plains to pass,
He filled the valleys with sweet green grass.

He made the nights so dark and cold,
the deserts He filled with sands of gold,
He made the sun's warmth the plants to grow,
He gave man wisdom which grains to sow.

He gave to mankind the symphony of life,
from the thunder of drums to the breeze of the fife;
the rippling streams, the roaring waterfalls
made music to accompany the wild bird calls..

When day is done and over the horizon the setting sun drops,
this is the cue for the moon and stars out of the heaven to pop;
now falls the soft black velvet, the final curtain of night,
for the music of the ocean and the breeze in the trees is infinite.

Denis R.H. Teal.

THE LIGHT OF THE WORLD

Painting by William Holman Hunt 1853

I stand in front of this painting mesmerised,
the crowned central figure holds my gaze,
the low-held lantern glows mystically,
casting dancing shadows that creep upwards,
the rich golds, bright oranges and muted greens of His robe
leap excitedly, flickering, contained within a warm soft brown cloak.

My eyes glide upwards, guided by the lantern,
to a still, shadowy gentle face, looking out at the world.

His eyes secretly seek mine, holding my gaze,
capturing me, inviting me into His world,
an unknown world of love, peace.
Calling to me, "Enter, enter into the spirit of the painting."

All this in contrast to the darkness surrounding Him,
silent, sinister black, suspended within an impenetrable wood,
tree trunks thickly wound angrily around each other,
quarrelling, choking, blocking out any light,
tangled weeds, decaying fruit block the door;
there is no entry outside, no handle, no escape.
He – patiently knocking at the door – waits.

Still he knocks patiently, until I hear and see His message,
"Come into My Light, and all that I offer,
a world of peace, love and life never-ending;
break free from the bleak darkness,
open the door, let the darkness crumble away."
I turn the handle inside, and know my soul is free.
He is standing, still, waiting – it is for me he is waiting.

Moyra Taylor.

SELF ESTEAM

The big picture hidden
behind the blurred vision
smudged clarity
vague suggestion of foggy reality
wet droplets falling
surface perspiring
the heat conspiring
with dampness to mislead.
A condensation creation.

Finger trails through moisture
creating meandering rivers;
now palm follows
swiping blurred vision
clearing vague suggestion
revealing reflected reality –
but at what ruinous cost?
Perspiring perception now lost.
Suddenly it all becomes clear –
and I long for the concealing mist!

Maggie McGladdery.

THE TAPESTRY OF LIFE

As we skip through the green pastures of life as a child
heading for a future where the climate can be cold or mild,
the mountains of happiness, the rivers of tears,
the valley of nights with black velvet fears,
the distant views hidden by the smoke-screen of time,
the current of life carrying us on with neither reason nor rhyme.

As we walk with ease on the shores of our rolling seas,
or struggling over rocky crags where eagles nest with their killer clees;
differences can be solved with handshakes and smiles;
arguments can be won with wit and with wiles.

No matter if your shadow points east, west, north or south,
you don't reason with a tiger when it has your head in its mouth!

Denis R.H. Teal.

BROMYARD POETS' CHRISTMAS DINNER

SYRUP TO THE HEART

Tonight we shall hear lines that will bring a smile or a tear
whilst enjoying coffee, red wine, or a glass of cold beer;
a verse from professionals, or the work of a beginner,
all around the table of our Group's Christmas Dinner.

We all meet tonight in this hostelry so grand
to enjoy the finest cuisine in all the land,
in this grand old room of good English oak
harvested from our ancient forests under oxen's yoke.

The wood being shaped by men using basic tools
with skills learned from their dads, not fancy schools;
the walls of stone and timber so strong and stout,
over the centuries keeping the elements and trouble out.

On leaving tonight full of food and good cheer,
with hopes and aspirations for the forthcoming year
as greetings are shared as we all depart
after discovering good verse is like syrup to the heart.

Denis R.H. Teal.

ABOUT THE POETS

Charles Gordon Clark and Thalia Gordon Clark. We were introduced to poetry at home and in our education. It has been a continual element in our lives. Poems learnt by heart have remained in our minds for use whenever the occasion arose.

Sadly Charles died earlier this year. Every one realised that we had a very learned man and poet amongst us and miss his knowledge and wisdom. He was a special man.

Bryony Cullum. Originally just a reader and listener my involvement has evolved into sharing poetry with young and old as well as those in between.

Jane Dallow. I enjoy poetry and over recent years have taken to expressing some of my thoughts and feelings by writing my own. I was born in Herefordshire and have lived here all my life. I was lucky to marry a Herefordshire man and to have 2 daughters. Without the support and encouragement of the Bromyard poetry group I doubt whether I should have become involved with poetry.

Margaret Dallow. Along with directing plays and taking art lessons I enjoy poetry and still wield comb and scissors.

Josie Ann Dolan,(nee Redfern.) Ann's education was in catering. In later life and a literary course at Cardiff University she returned to Bromyard and used her literary talents in script writing and poetry. She was passionate about Bromyard and its community.

John Elmes. Sadly John died in 2017. He was a wonderful story teller, widely travelled and had a gift for showing us the abundant life of the countryside in a way appreciated by the BBC and the many groups to whom he read his poetry. Margaret was proud to accept a beautifully turned wooden gavel, another of his remarkable skills, to keep us in order.

Peter Holliday. I was born in Hereford and have lived in Welsh Border Country for almost 50 years. I was Leominster's Librarian for more than 20 years. I lecture widely on local history. I strive to write good poetry with the star of Shamus Heaney before me.

Dorothy Kennedy. Our Dad used to read poetry to us. A favourite of mine was The Centurion's Tale by Rudyard Kipling. He also recited Julius Caesar to us. I loved Mum's poetry book The Golden Staircase. I can still remember poems learnt at primary school. O level poetry lessons were heaven.

Judy Malet. Having lived in England, Scotland, India and Africa, I have always wanted to "belong" somewhere. Herefordshire has given me that wish and the time to write thoughts in poems.

Maggie McGladdery. Since retiring I have returned to painting but I am also enjoying my discovery of painting with words.

John Pare. This book contains my first voluntary piece of writing: I started with nursery rhymes! Only when I retired and dug out notebooks did I realise how much I had written in between. Writing poetry has helped me enormously and I now have my own muse as well.

Rosemarie Powell. A staunch admirer of my sister Ann Dolan's poetry I was inspired and encouraged to start writing my own. I gained motivation on visiting Antigua in 2012/2013. I hope you enjoy this collection from a very different world.

Moyra Taylor. I have always loved poetry, writing a little off and on throughout the years. I feel so lucky to be a member of poetry for Pleasure, which has inspired me to KEEP WRITING!

Denis, R.H. Teal. I was born at Kyrebach, Thornbury. On leaving school at 15, I became a van boy for Goldings' hardware. I trained as a medic in the R.A.F. for my National Service. Married with 4 children, I managed the largest supermarket in Herefordshire, at the time, but left to work less hours at a pet shop in Worcester until 1998, when I retired and became photographer for the Bromyard Gala and Off the Record. In spite of my meagre education I enjoy poetry and have written some poems.

Mary Wakefield Jones. Living a busy farming life I find time occasionally to dash off a poem and I enjoy listening to and reading poetry.

ILLUSTRATIONS/ART WORK by

Jane Dallow, 80

Maggie McGladdery, 35, 44, 78, 97

Denis R.H. Teal, cover, 20, 23, 128

Arthur Lowe, 37, 38, 41, 71

William Holman Hunt, 123

Anon, 75

Index of poets